Dear Parent:
Your child's love of reading starts here!

Every child learns to read in a different way and at his or her own speed. Some go back and forth between reading levels and read favorite books again and again. Others read through each level in order. You can help your young reader improve and become more confident by encouraging his or her own interests and abilities. From books your child reads with you to the first books he or she reads alone, there are I Can Read Books for every stage of reading:

SHARED READING
Basic language, word repetition, and whimsical illustrations, ideal for sharing with your emergent reader

BEGINNING READING
Short sentences, familiar words, and simple concepts for children eager to read on their own

READING WITH HELP
Engaging stories, longer sentences, and language play for developing readers

READING ALONE
Complex plots, challenging vocabulary, and high-interest topics for the independent reader

ADVANCED READING
Short paragraphs, chapters, and exciting themes for the perfect bridge to chapter books

I Can Read Books have introduced children to the joy of reading since 1957. Featuring award-winning authors and illustrators and a fabulous cast of beloved characters, I Can Read Books set the standard for beginning readers.

A lifetime of discovery begins with the magical words **"I Can Read!"**

Visit www.icanread.com for information
on enriching your child's reading experience.

For Mr. Heller, who taught me to love history.
—S.A.

Your love for each other and the joy you share
have left fingerprints on my heart.
Thank you Nancy and Uwe, this book is for you.
—C.K.

Special thanks to Mount Vernon staffers Mary Thompson and Sarah Myers
for their valuable assistance, and to American History teacher Jon Willson
of the Taft School.

Picture Credits
The following photographs, paintings, and engravings are © Getty images: page 28, *Washington's Marriage*
by Junius Brutus Stearns; *Surrender of Cornwallis at Yorktown* by John Trumbull; page 29, *Washington at
Home*; slave quarters at Mount Vernon; page 30, James Armistead Lafayette; Page 33, portrait of George
Washington.

The following images are courtesy of the Library of Congress: page 31, page from the Culper codebook;
engraving of George Washington with dogs at Mount Vernon by Thomas Oldham Barlow.

I Can Read Book® is a trademark of HarperCollins Publishers.

Library of Congress Control Number: 2017939000
ISBN 978-0-06-243267-4 (trade bdg.) — ISBN 978-0-06-243266-7—(pbk.)

Book design by Jeff Shake

17 18 19 20 21 SCP 10 9 8 7 6 5 4 3 2 1

❖ First Edition

I Can Read!™

READING 2 WITH HELP

GEORGE WASHINGTON
The First President

by Sarah Albee
pictures by Chin Ko

HARPER
An Imprint of HarperCollinsPublishers

In 1776, colonists in America
declared independence from Britain.
The two sides fought a war called
the American Revolution.

George Washington was the general
who led the American army.
He was brave, honest, and fair.
The war lasted eight years.
The Americans finally won.

America was a new country!

But who would lead it?

Everyone knew the answer:

George Washington, of course.

Should he be a king?

Should he be a president?

But George shocked everyone.

He did not want to be a king.

He did not want to be a president.

"I retire," he said.

In England, King George was shocked.

In France, King Louis was shocked.

Everyone was shocked.

No one gave up power by choice!

But George Washington did.

Who was this man who said no thanks?

George was born in Virginia in 1732.

When George was eleven,

his father died.

George was close to

his half-brother, Lawrence.

When George was nineteen,

Lawrence died.

George inherited a big farm.

It was called Mount Vernon.

America was still part of Britain.

The French and British both wanted

more land in North America.

Young George was sent west

to claim more land for Great Britain.

With no roads, George traveled

by horse, by raft, and on foot.

But when he finally arrived,

French soldiers were already there.

They refused to leave.

George returned to Virginia.

He wrote about his trip.

The French king was not happy.

He wanted that land for France.

The French and British went to war.

Some native people sided with France,

so British colonists called it

the French and Indian War.

Young George was made a major.
He and his men fought bravely
on the side of Great Britain.
After many years, Great Britain won.
But the war had been expensive.

When he was twenty-six,

George met Martha Custis.

She was barely five feet tall.

He was nearly six foot three.

Martha was a rich widow.

George was brave and handsome.

She had two small children.

He loved children.

They got married.

The British wanted the colonists to help
pay for the French and Indian war.
The British raised taxes.
They passed unfair laws.
(At least the Americans thought so.)

Finally, the colonists had enough.

That's why the revolution began.

That's when Washington took command.

British soldiers were well trained.

They wore fine red coats.

American soldiers were untrained.

They wore shabby uniforms.

With some help from the French,
the Americans won many battles.
The British surrendered.
General George Washington was
the most famous man in America.

George helped create a plan

for a new government.

It was called the Constitution.

People begged George not to retire.

At last, he agreed to be President.

George had to figure out

how to lead a new country.

"I walk on untrodden ground,"

he said.

Martha became the first First Lady.

George chose smart people

to help him.

Together they formed a government.

The new Congress made wise laws.

New coins were minted.

A new country was created.

Everyone begged George

to run for president a second time.

He served four more years.

But he said no to a third time.

The people should choose a new leader.

George knew what was best

for the new country.

A few years after he retired,
George died at home, in Virginia.
Thomas Jefferson called him
"a wise, a good, and a great man."

Timeline

1730

1732
Washington is born.

1743
Washington's father dies.

1740

1751
Washington's half-brother, Lawrence, dies.

1753
Washington travels west to claim new land for Great Britain.

1754
The French and Indian War begins.

1750

1759
Washington marries Martha Dandridge Custis.

1760

1775
The American Revolution begins. Washington takes command of the American army.

1770

1781
The British surrender at Yorktown, Virginia.

1780

1783
America and Great Britain sign a peace treaty. The war is over.

1789
Washington is elected president.

1790

1797
Washington steps down as president.

1799
Washington dies of a throat infection.

1802
Martha Washington dies.

1800

George and Martha enslaved many people.

George Washington owned 316 people when he died. They were mostly of African origin. He did not treat them especially kindly. It was a very prejudiced time.

George Washington's views on slavery changed over time. He grew more and more troubled by slavery. In his will, he freed many of his slaves.

Inside slave quarters at Mount Vernon.

At Mount Vernon, enslaved people without families lived in rooms with bunk beds, like this one. The large space was heated by a single fireplace at one end of the room. The fireplace was also used for cooking. The room would have been very cold in the winter and hot in the summer.

During the American Revolution, George Washington used many spies.

Some seemed like ordinary merchants, tailors, and farmers. Some were women. Others were African American. The spies helped Washington learn information about British battle plans and strategies.

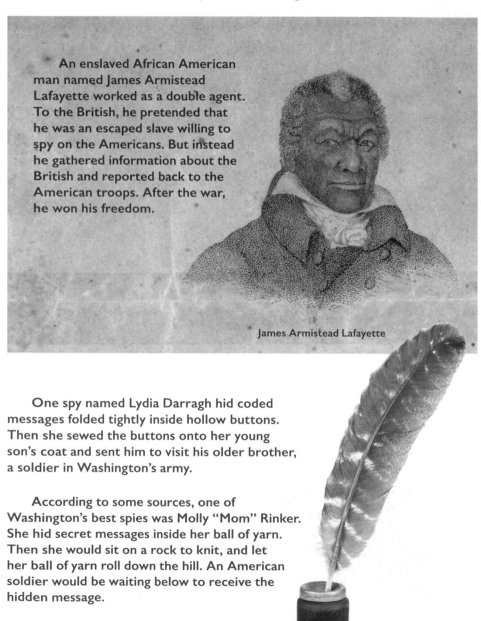

An enslaved African American man named James Armistead Lafayette worked as a double agent. To the British, he pretended that he was an escaped slave willing to spy on the Americans. But instead he gathered information about the British and reported back to the American troops. After the war, he won his freedom.

James Armistead Lafayette

One spy named Lydia Darragh hid coded messages folded tightly inside hollow buttons. Then she sewed the buttons onto her young son's coat and sent him to visit his older brother, a soldier in Washington's army.

According to some sources, one of Washington's best spies was Molly "Mom" Rinker. She hid secret messages inside her ball of yarn. Then she would sit on a rock to knit, and let her ball of yarn roll down the hill. An American soldier would be waiting below to receive the hidden message.

Here's a page of a codebook used by Washington's special spy ring. Some names were represented by numbers. General Washington was "711." Some numbers were represented by letters. The year 1779 might be written as "ennq."

Sometimes Washington's spies wrote in invisible ink between the lines of books, using the code number system.

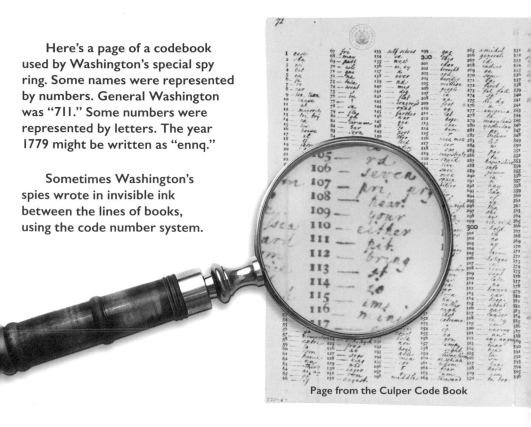

Page from the Culper Code Book

George and Martha Washington loved dogs.

George had hunting dogs named Sweetlips, Tipsy, Mopsey, and Ragman. The Washingtons had a carriage dog named Madame Moose. Many other kinds of dogs also lived at Mount Vernon. Several terriers guarded the stores of flour and grain, chasing away mice and rats.

George Washington standing on the patio at Mount Vernon.

What did George Washington look like?

George Washington stood much taller than most men for his time. He may have been as tall as six foot three.

Many men wore wigs in colonial America. George Washington did not wear a wig, but he did put powder in his hair to make it white. That was the fashion at the time.

George Washington had terrible trouble with his teeth. One by one, they had to be pulled out. By the time he was president, he had just one tooth left in his mouth. He had several pairs of false teeth. Some were made of hippopotamus teeth, gold, and lead. They gave him a lumpy-looking mouth. It was difficult for him to smile without having his teeth pop out.

Find Out More

Visit www.mountvernon.org or go see Mount Vernon in person. It's close to Washington, DC.

Visit the Smithsonian National Museum of African American History and Culture in Washington, DC (*http://nmaahc.si.edu*).

Visit Valley Forge National Historical Park in Montgomery County, Pennsylvania (or online at *www.valleyforge.org*).